T0020948

OUR LADY'S WARDROBE

Anthony DeStefano

Illustrated by Juliana Kolesova

SOPHIA INSTITUTE PRESS
Manchester, NH

SOPHIA
INSTITUTE PRESS

Text Copyright © 2020 by Anthony DeStefano
Images Copyright © 2020 by Juliana Kolesova

Printed in the United States of America.

Sophia Institute Press®
Box 5284, Manchester, NH 03108
1-800-888-9344

www.SophiaInstitute.com
Sophia Institute Press® is a registered trademark of Sophia Institute.

No part of this book may be reproduced, stored in a retrieval system, or transmitted in any form, or by any means, electronic, mechanical, photocopying, or otherwise, without the prior written permission of the publisher, except by a reviewer, who may quote brief passages in a review.

Library of Congress Control Number: 2020932243

This book is dedicated to Our Lady,
Queen of the Most Holy Rosary.
— *Anthony DeStefano*

Our Lady leads us to the Lord;
that's what she's always done.
She gave us Jesus Christ the King,
God's one and only Son.

But when Our Lady lived on Earth,
humble, meek, and poor,
all her clothes could fit inside
a tiny little drawer.

OUR LADY
OF NAZARETH

So visiting her cousin's house,
the handmaid of the Lord
could only wear a handmade dress,
tied with a simple cord.

But now in Heaven Mary has
a mansion by the sea,
with a wardrobe filled with clothes
of great variety.

And when she sometimes visits us
she picks her clothes with care.
According to her travel plans
she chooses what to wear.

On Mount Carmel she held her Son,
all dressed in tan and brown.
She clasped a tiny scapular
and wore a golden crown.

OUR LADY
OF MOUNT CARMEL

She formed a great community
that still exists today,
of holy monks and holy nuns
who serve the poor and pray.

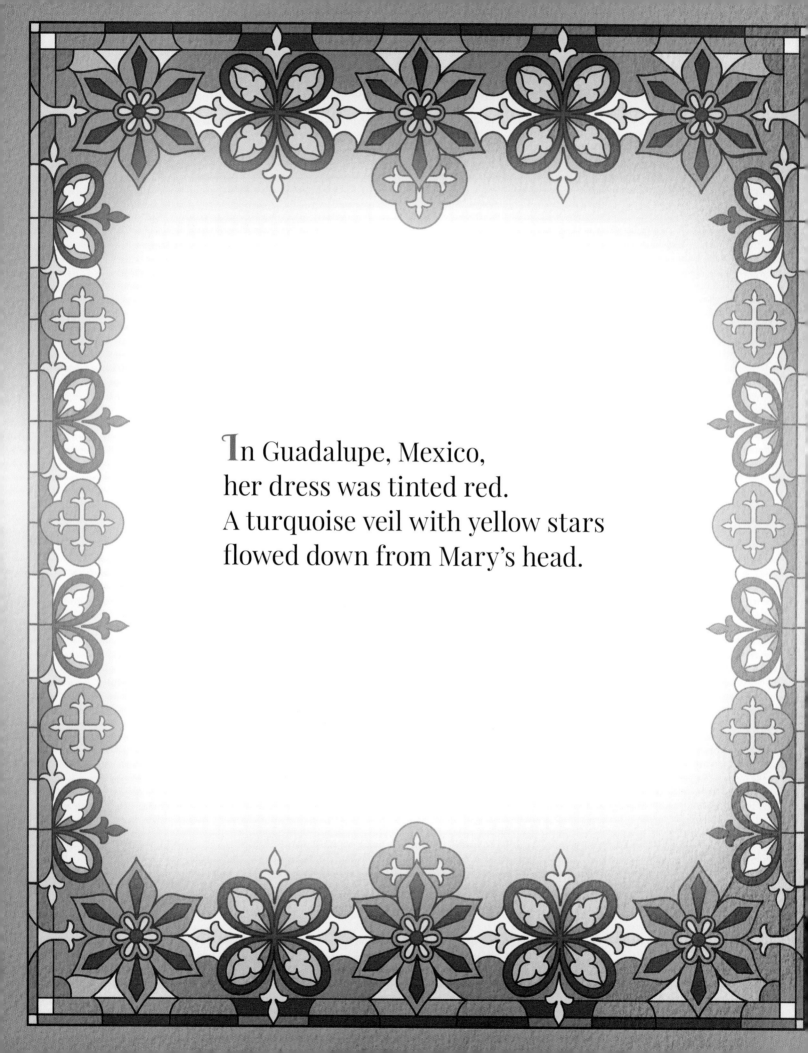

In Guadalupe, Mexico,
her dress was tinted red.
A turquoise veil with yellow stars
flowed down from Mary's head.

She put some roses in a cloak,
arranged them lovingly,
and left her sacred image there,
magnificent to see.

In Paris, standing on a globe
and clad in blue and white,
her hands stretched out and
   from her rings
came dazzling rays of light.

On the medal:

O MARY CONCEIVED WITHOUT SIN PRAY FOR US WHO HAVE RECOURSE TO THEE

1830

She asked to have a medal made
and worn by everyone;
then miracles of every kind
were granted by her Son.

In Ireland Our Lady dressed
in shades of white and green,
to show that she would always be
the Emerald Isle's Queen.

OUR LADY
OF KNOCK

She stood in silence in the night
and uttered not a word.
The howling wind and falling rain
were all that could be heard.

She wore for little Bernadette—
a French girl pure and sweet—
a frilly veil, a long blue sash,
and roses on her feet.

OUR LADY
OF LOURDES

She came from out a grotto
and the little French girl kneeled;
then Mary made a fountain spring
where all the sick were healed.

In Fatima Our Lady stood
upon a holly tree.
She dressed in white
    like crystal light
and held a rosary.

She then performed a miracle,
well-known in history:
the sun came down and spun around
and danced for all to see.

No matter what Our Lady does and where Our Lady goes,
she always takes the time to wear the most amazing clothes.
Her clothes are proof that Heaven is a truly wondrous place—
a land of beauty, life, and love and joy and truth and grace.

The Queen of Angels smiles now,
from Heaven up above.
Her face is so delightful
and her heart so full of love.

She stands there shining like the sun,
in robes of blue and red;
a crown of twelve bright sparkling stars
she wears upon her head

O Mary, Queen Immaculate,
please help us love your Son.
Please help us trust and serve Him
till our life on Earth is done.

The End

OUR LADY
QUEEN OF THE ANGELS

*Three things you can do
for Jesus and His mother!*

If you wear a scapular
and Mary's medal too,
and pray the Rosary every day,
God's grace is promised you.

The Scapular

"a Sign of Salvation," Our Lady of Mt. Carmel to St. Simon Stock – 1251

"Whosoever dies clothed in this Scapular shall not suffer eternal fire." The Scapular Promise from Our Lady of Mt. Carmel

M

The Miraculous Medal

O MARY CONCEIVED WITHOUT SIN PRAY FOR US WHO HAVE RECOURSE TO THEE 1830

The Rosary

Hail Mary,
full of grace.
The Lord is with thee.
Blessed art thou
amongst women,
and blessed is the fruit
of thy womb, Jesus.
Holy Mary, Mother of God,
pray for us sinners,
now and at the hour
of our death.
Amen.

*Ave
Maria* ℳ *Salve
Regina*

The Scapular

"a Sign of Salvation,..."

Our Lady of Mt. Carmel to St. Simon Stock - 1251

"Whosoever dies clothed in this Scapular shall not suffer eternal fire." The Scapular Promise from Our Lady of Mt. Carmel

The Rosary

The Miraculous Medal

O MARY CONCEIVED WITHOUT SIN PRAY FOR US WHO HAVE RECOURSE TO THEE

1830

From the Bible

And a great sign appeared in heaven: A woman clothed with the sun, and the moon under her feet, and on her head a crown of twelve stars.

—Revelation 12:1 (DRA)

In the sixth month the angel Gabriel was sent from God to a city of Galilee named Nazareth, to a virgin betrothed to a man whose name was Joseph, of the house of David; and the virgin's name was Mary. And he came to her and said, "Hail, full of grace, the Lord is with you! ... Do not be afraid, Mary, for you have found favor with God. And behold, you will conceive in your womb and bear a son, and you shall call his name Jesus."

—Luke 1:26–28, 30–31 (RSVCE)

And Mary said: "Behold the handmaid of the Lord; be it done to me according to thy word." And the angel departed from her.

—Luke 1:38 (DRA)